SAM KAN

Financial Statements Secrets For Small Business Owners

Crack the code of ratio analysis, and improve the cashflow like a CFO, even if you have zero experience

This book was professionally typeset on Reedsy.
Find out more at reedsy.com

Contents

Introduction

I have a lot of respect for small business owners. They wear many hats to keep their businesses running smoothly, acting as investors, CEOs, CFOs, marketers, IT personnel, human resources, and business operators, among other roles. They try their best to grow their businesses and make them profitable.

However, their efforts may translate to something other than a proportional return on investment. Many business owners need more cash flow in their businesses. They hope that working harder and longer hours will solve the issue. Still, these hopes are dashed every time payday arrives, or certain bills are due because the business lacks sufficient cash.

I understand this feeling because I have been there. I started my small business about 17 years ago. I was passionate about my accounting services. However, the busyness of the business distracted me from analyzing its financial health. Despite being a Certified Public Accountant (CPA), I am embarrassed to tell you I used to prepare my financial reports only to file tax returns. I should have used my accounting knowledge to improve my business. I continued to work hard and long hours (yes, I used to get up at 3 am to start working) until one day, I discovered I did not have enough cash to meet payroll.

At that time, I had no idea what the problem was and felt completely lost. I thought my business was profitable and was surprised to discover that my cash flow was struggling.

If the business could have been better, why was I so busy? I felt stuck, lost, and ashamed when I could not make ends meet.

My mindset shifted at that point. I realized I was like an orchestra conductor who had left my conductor spot to try and play the musical instruments by myself. I would not be able to listen to the music from other musicians clearly as the volume of certain parts could be out of balance. Other musicians couldn't play with good timing when they couldn't see the guide from the conductor.

One of the significant roles of the conductor is to oversee the orchestra's performance and take actions to guide the musicians on the right track.

Similarly, as a small business owner, I must oversee every aspect of my accounting business.

I needed to slow down and use financial reports to monitor the business's financial health.

Since then, I have done the bookkeeping monthly and prepared the financial statements timely. I have developed several analytical strategies and key performance indicators (KPIs) to track my business using timely monthly financial reports. My business's cash flow and profit have improved, setting a good foundation for continued growth. After working as the CFO of my company, my revenue grew to 7 digits in 3 years and another 7 digits in the following 2 years.

Thanks to my accounting background, I am fortunate to have learned techniques for doing so. Sharing my knowledge and helping other business owners use financial reports like a CFO has become my passion.

This book can be your practical guide to using financial statements like a CFO. There are many approaches to analyzing financial information, and CFOs can play many roles. We will focus on a few that can quickly help you improve profitability in less than 12 months.

We will first cover the method of financial analysis in Chapter 1. This vital chapter defines how we perform analysis by "ERA."

Chapter 2 could be optional if you already understand the essential components of the financial statements.

We will then examine some examples to see how numbers can be converted into cash. The examples were from my bookkeeping clients. However, I changed the number, clients' names, and some of their industries to protect their privacy.

Before we embark on this journey together, let me introduce myself a little more. I started my career as a bookkeeper about 20 years ago. I became a CPA and started my own practice in my basement in 2006 when my daughter was born.

In 2008, my son was born. As a father of two young children, it was impossible to nurture my new business without my wife's support. She is always very understanding and encouraging whenever I need to work long hours or be away from home for business trips.

As mentioned above, running the business was stressful because of the cash flow pressure. I would have given up if the situation had not improved. After I have learned how I made informed decisions from the ratio analysis, like a CFO, I am eager to share with other small business owners. Thus bookkeeping services have become my firm's core business.

My team is currently helping about 200 small businesses with monthly bookkeeping. I am fortunate to witness the growth of my client's businesses. It is an honor for my team to know that the timely financial reports we prepare are important to their success.

Chapter 1 - Analytics

When you look at your car dashboard, it provides you with a lot of information, such as speed, engine light, temperature, tire pressure, fuel consumption, seat belt indicator, and more. However, simply reading this data is not a comprehensive analysis. For instance, let's say you know that your vehicle's gas mileage is 300 miles for a full tank, which has a capacity of around 10 gallons.

One day, you fill up the gas tank completely, and the gas gauge shows empty after driving 200 miles, according to the odometer. If you only fill up with more gas without thinking about why the gas tank was empty after the drive of 200 miles, you have yet to utilize the information. Knowing the data does not mean you have analyzed or used it yet. You may even calculate the ratio and know that the gas mileage of the last trip was 20 miles per gallon of gas, but this is still not analytic. This is merely a ratio calculation.

So what is analysis?

Here are the steps to follow, and I name the process as "ERA":

Expectation: Gas mileage is 300 miles per 10 gallons of gas (full tank).

5

You set this expectation based on the vehicle's historical performance and the vehicle's specifications.

Reality check: The vehicle has traveled only 200 miles, and the gas tank is almost empty. The ratio is 20 miles per gallon, while your expected gas mileage is 30 miles per gallon. There is a discrepancy between the actual performance and the desired outcome, so it leads to the final step below.

Action: Initiate an investigation to determine the cause. You should check if the oil and air filters are too dirty, if the air conditioner is working properly, if the tire pressure is adequate, etc. After the investigation, say you find out the oil and air filters are too dirty, you take the necessary action to change them to improve gas mileage on the next trip. This could lead to better alignment with your expectations and help ensure the vehicle performs at its best.

By performing the analysis, you can identify which areas do not align with your expectations. Thus, you will take the necessary actions to improve the situation.

From the exercise above, I would like to introduce you to the analytic concept using "ERA."

"ERA" stands for "Expectation," "Reality Check," and "Action." This mnemonic represents the basic analytics elements critical for making informed decisions based on data.

Expectation:

Expectation refers to the desired or expected outcome you want to see.

The first step of the data analysis process is clearly understanding what you are trying to achieve. You must have the expectation to measure if the outcome is on track or if additional action is needed.

The expectation for your financial ratios could be derived from different sources. It could be from the historical data in prior years, which provides the trend of your business. It could be from the news. For instance, you should expect the salary expense to increase with the raise in the minimum wage. It could be from your business knowledge, say you expect to spend more money on repairs when your equipment is getting old.

Reality Check:

This step involves using the actual data to present them with the relevant information and then using the information to compare with the expectations. In financial analysis, the financial figures (data) will be used in calculating specific ratios (relevant information) for the users of the financial statements to compare with the expectations. Suppose the comparison shows a discrepancy to the expected outcome. In that case, it will lead to the final step in the analysis described below.

Action:

Before taking any action based on the insight of the reality check, we should start by brainstorming the reasons for the discrepancies. After the potential causes of the issues are identified and a thorough investigation is done, the related action plans can be developed to address the problems. The action plan could involve changing the operating process, implementing new strategies, or adjusting goals to align better with the data.

This book will examine essential ratios from financial reports and perform financial analysis using "ERA." This approach will help you make sense of the numbers and extract meaningful insights from financial data.

Chapter 2 - Basic components

B efore using "ERA" to perform financial analysis, let's understand the basic components of the Income Statement and Balance Sheet.

Part 1: Income Statement

This statement is also known as the Statement of Profit and Loss or P&L. It summarizes the business's operating results over time. The major components of the income statement are as follows:

Revenue
Less: Cost of Goods Sold
= Gross Profit

Less: Operating Expenses
= Operating Income / Loss

Less: Income Tax
=Net Income / Loss

Figure 2.1

Note: we skipped other non-operational income/expenses in the above presentation for simplicity.

Revenue

Revenue, also sometimes referred to as income or sales, is the money earned by the business from customers through rendering services or selling products. It is presented as the net amount, which means it's after returns, discounts, and sales tax.

Cost of Goods Sold

The Cost of Goods Sold is not equal to the purchase of goods. The purchase of goods is reported as inventory in the Balance Sheet. It will be reported as the cost of goods sold once the sales are recognized.

For example, if you purchase one unit of goods for $10 in January 20XX, and the unit is sold in February 20XX for $25, the income statements of January 20XX and February 20XX will be presented as follows:

	For the month ended January 31, 20XX	For the month ended February 28, 20XX
Revenue	$ -	$25
Cost of Goods sold	-	10
Gross Profit	$ -	$15

Figure 2.2

You may be wondering where we record the purchase of $10 in January

20XX. It's not in the income statement. It's booked to "Inventory" in the Balance Sheet.

Gross Profit

Gross profit is calculated by subtracting the cost of goods sold from the revenue. This is an important component in the income statement because it's the amount the business can pay for all the operating expenses and cover the net profit.

Operating Expenses

Operating expenses are the expenses incurred in operating the business. It is also referred to as "Overhead." Some also present the operating expenses as Selling, General, and Administrative (SG&A).

For General and Administrative expenses, I usually break them down into the following four categories:

- Selling expenses, which include marketing, advertising, salaries related to sales, shipping fees, etc.
- Personnel expenses include salary and wages, payroll tax, employee benefits, training, etc.
- Occupancy expenses include rent, utilities, building insurance, telephone, internet, repair, maintenance, etc.
- Other general and administrative expenses include supplies, insurance, legal and accounting fees, software, travel, depreciation, amortization, bank charges, interest, research & development, etc.

I like the above breakdown because personnel expenses are usually the major portion of business operating expenses. It is helpful to group all the personnel expenses and compare them to the sales.

Occupancy expenses are an important group for many businesses because they incur many fixed operating expenses regardless of sales results. For instance, the company will need to pay for rent, building maintenance, building insurance, telephone, internet, etc., even if no sales are generated in a particular month. Unlike variable operating expenses, they are hard to reduce when sales are not good because the occupancy expense often comes with commitment. For instance, if the business signs a lease for five years with a monthly rent of $5,000, the commitment of the rent in each of the following five years will be $60,000 per year. This obligation is not a liability as the expense has yet to be incurred.

Income Tax

In the United States, some businesses operate as pass-through entities, such as S-corporations and LLCs. This means income tax is passed through to the individual level, resulting in no or low-income tax at the business level. Nevertheless, it's good practice to evaluate the net profit (profit after tax) by hypothetically assessing the effective tax rate to understand how much money should be set aside for estimated tax payments.

Net Income

Net income, also referred to as net profit, is the difference between operating income and income tax, assuming there are no other income / other expenses.

Part 2: Balance Sheet

The Balance Sheet reports the assets, liabilities, and equity of a business at a specific point in time. It provides a snapshot of the business's financial position, including how much it owns in assets, owes in liabilities, and has in working capital.

Assets include cash, accounts receivable, inventory, property, and equipment, among other items.

Cash includes petty cash and bank accounts and is essential for a business's survival.

Accounts receivable is the amount owed to the company by customers. Preparing an accounts receivable aging report helps identify which customers owe the company for over 90 days.

Inventory is the unsold goods held by the business. It is closely related to the cost of goods sold account since sold inventory is converted to the cost of goods sold in the income statement once sales are recognized. Therefore, it's important to count the ending inventory monthly, or at least annually, to capture the cost of goods sold accurately. An inventory worksheet can help identify slow-moving items that may become obsolete, and sales promotions can be used to sell them quickly. The formula of inventory associated with the cost of goods sold (COGS) is as follows:

COGS = Beginning inventory + Purchases - Ending inventory

Property and equipment, also known as fixed assets, are expected to benefit the company over a year. This category includes accumulated depreciation and amortization, which help the users of the financial statements determine the net book value. Net book value is the difference between the historical cost of the property and the accumulated depreciation. The net book value is not affected by the change in the fair market value.

Liabilities include accounts payable, loans, and tax payable.

Accounts payable is the amount owed to vendors and is typically non-interest bearing, usually due within 30 days.

Loan payable is divided into current and long-term portions. The current portion is the debt due within the next 12 months, and the business needs to know this information to prepare for cash flow requirements.

Tax payable includes income tax, sales tax, payroll tax, and other taxes owed.

Equity is the difference between assets and liabilities and represents the working capital available to the business.

You can also get the balance of equity from another angle. It's the sum of shareholders' contributions minus all distributions plus all profits or losses from the business's inception to the balance sheet date.

In conclusion, understanding the basic components of the Income Statement and Balance Sheet helps perform financial analysis effectively. By analyzing financial statements, business owners can gain valuable insights into their business's financial health, make informed decisions, and take steps to improve profitability and growth.

For the rest of this book, we will use "ERA" (Expectation, Realty Check, Action) to perform the financial analysis to improve the cash flow.

Chapter 3 - Gross Profit Margin

L et's discuss a vital ratio: Gross Profit Margin.

As discussed in the last chapter, gross profit is the difference between revenue and cost of goods sold. Gross Profit Margin is the percentage of gross profit to revenue.

The formula for Gross Profit Margin is as follows:

$$\text{Gross profit} = \text{Revenue} - \text{Cost}$$

$$\text{Gross profit margin} = (\text{Revenue} - \text{cost}) / \text{Revenue} * 100\%$$

As we have learned from Chapter 1, we cannot just rely on the formula and perform the ratio calculations; we need to complete the analysis by "ERA."

Here are some case studies from my accounting practice. I have changed the names, numbers, and even industries to protect their privacy. Even if you are not in the same industry, you can still apply the logic and thought processes to your business.

Daisy - a restaurant owner

Here is an example of how we helped a restaurant owner, Daisy, with her business. Our team has been performing monthly bookkeeping for Daisy's bar and grill restaurant since she built it from scratch about 9 years ago. We noticed that her gross profit margin had decreased compared to the prior years. We contacted her to perform the analysis based on "ERA" together.

When we informed Daisy about the decrease in gross profit margin, she initially wasn't interested in it as she thought it was just a temporary fluctuation. Daisy's key performance indicator for her business was the cash balance in the bank account. She felt the company was running fine as long as she had enough cash in the bank.

However, we explained to her that the decrease in gross profit margin could affect her cash flow by about $100,000 in the next 12 to 18 months. This message drew her attention, and we started the analysis process.

a. Expectation

Sam: "What is your gross profit margin?"

Daisy: "Hmm... I don't know."

Sam: "Don't worry. Did you make any significant changes to the menu?"

Daisy: "Nope."

Sam: "Okay, so I think the average gross profit margin in the first 4 years will be a good way to set our expectations."

The average ratio was 70% in the first four years, which was in line with other restaurants in the industry. We asked if Daisy agreed, and she said it looked good.

b. Reality Check

Sam: "Based on the income statement, your quarterly gross profit margin is about 67%. It was about the same in the last two quarters, which means it has been 3 quarters in a row reporting the reduction in gross profit margin."

Daisy: "I see. Is it still profitable?"

Sam: "Yes, your business is still profitable. The drop in gross profit margin is just something worth our attention to improve the business. The trend of the decrease started two years ago."

Daisy: "Why did 3% reduce the gross profit margin in the last 3 quarters?"

Sam: "We don't know the reason yet. We know the cash flow would have been about $54,000 more if the gross margin were 70% in the last three quarters."

(Note: The sales for the 9 months ended September 30, 20XX, was about $1,800,000 in Daisy's restaurant, so a 3% decrease in gross profit margin represented about $54,000, $1,800,000 * 3%, drop in gross profit)

Daisy: "Wow, that's a lot of money. How did you come up with this number?"

Sam: "Your projected sales are about $2,400,000 annually, about

$1,800,000 for 3 quarters. A 3% reduction in gross profit margin represents about a $54,000 drop. This is just historical data from the past. If no corrective action is taken, the situation could worsen."

Daisy: "Can you help me fix it?"

Sam: "Let's brainstorm the cause and solution together."

c. Action

Sam: "Did you change your chef this year, and did he increase the portion size of the dishes?"

Daisy: "No, we've been using the same chef for four years, and our portion sizes have stayed about the same. However, we did change our bartender earlier this year. I'm unsure if he's been pouring more wine and liquor for our customers."

Sam: "That's good to know. One of the action items will be to investigate if your bartender is giving out too many free drinks in exchange for tips. You may want to inform your bartenders, standardize drink portions, and the policy about when they could give out free drinks. Even a 30% increase in portion size could reduce your gross profit margin from 70% to 61% in drinks. It could represent a reduction of approximately $50,000 in gross profit, given that drinks account for about 30% of your overall sales."

[Note: if the sales for the 9 months were about $1,800,000, 30% of the sales were related to the drinks, it was $540,000 ($1,800,000 * 30%) sales in the drink. The expected gross profit should be $378,000, and the drinks cost should be $162,000. However, if the cost of drinks were increased by 30% because of the more significant portion or excessive free drinks given, the gross profit would be reduced to $329,400 [$540,000 - $162,000 * (1+30%)], which is representing the reduction of $48,600 ($378,000-329,400).]

Daisy: "What about meal sales?

Sam: "You can do the same for meals and observe which side dishes are excessive and if the customers are generally unable to finish. However, the variance in your business in this area may not be significant. A 1 to 2% reduction in food waste would only save you $5,000 to $10,000 per year."

Daisy: "It's better than nothing! I'll definitely take a closer look at this area."

I could tell she was beginning to see the numbers in the income statement as cash.

Sam: "If you haven't significantly changed your menu, your vendor has increased prices by an average of 2.5% per year in the last three years. Have you adjusted your menu prices accordingly?"

Daisy: "Of course, we've adjusted our prices a few times in the last three years."

Sam: "What was the percentage change per year approximately?"

Daisy: "It's hard to say. We've just tried to keep up with inflation and added $1 to $2 to certain meals here and there. I haven't calculated the overall percentage changes."

Sam: "No problem. Your second action item is to track your point of sales reports in the last three years and determine the overall percentage changes in each year."

The meeting ended with two action items: (1) standardize the policy of drink portions and the policy of giving out free drinks; (2) investigate the percentage changes in menu prices in the last three years.

Daisy didn't call me back with her findings. I emailed her to ask if she had the results of her investigation.

Daisy was embarrassed: "I found that the last time I changed menu prices was a year before last year. It was about a 3% change in some items."

Sam: "Not bad! How about the years before that?"

Daisy: "I thought we had adjusted prices, but I was mistaken. I must have been too busy and forgot to make the adjustments."

Sam: "Don't worry. It's still early enough to identify the problem and adjust as soon as possible."

Daisy: "Sure. I'll adjust the selling price by 2.5% soon."

Sam: "I think you should increase it more since you've only adjusted once in the last three years. With the current year, you must make a one-time catch-up adjustment of about 7%. I know it's a big jump, so I recommend doing it more frequently in the future."

Daisy acknowledged my advice and stated that she would change the menu twice a year, once in the summer and once in the winter, to avoid upsetting her customers from now on. Daisy understood the customers should be okay with a slight adjustment at a time. However, the one-time catch-up of 7% proved to be a challenge.

I suggested that Daisy add new items and a few more combos to the menu, which might make the price changes less noticeable. Daisy was unsure but said she would discuss it further with her chef and appreciated my suggestions.

Sometimes, the situation cannot be fully resolved, and the expected ratios may need to be adjusted, as in this case, from 70% to 67%. However, it is essential to investigate the issue before giving up.

Daisy's gross profit margin improved to about 70% the following year. The further analysis helped her understand the issues better. The financial analysis provided a starting point for her to dig deeper.

Takeaway:

This case study demonstrates how the cash flow was improved by about $100,000 in less than 2 years when the gross profit margin was carefully monitored, and necessary action plans were implemented.

From the above analysis, Daisy found out she forgot to adjust the menu price despite the increase in the food cost, and the drink portion needed to be standardized when she had a new bartender.

Is your business's gross profit margin meet your desired outcome? If yes, do you have any idea to increase it further? On the other hand, do you know why the gross profit margin was lower than what you expected? I hope this case study has inspired your thought. Please take a break and calculate your business's gross profit margin from your income statement. Perform "ERA" and see what will come to your attention.

Sarah - a business owner of an e-commerce

a. Expectation:

Sam: "Hello, Sarah; how is your e-commerce business doing?"

Sarah: "Things are going well, but we're struggling with space issues in our warehouse. I was considering renting another warehouse to cope with our growing inventory."

Sam: "That's great news that your business is expanding. However, renting a new warehouse is a significant commitment and comes with additional overhead expenses like staffing, utilities, and equipment. Instead of making a decision based on a feeling of overcrowding, let's use financial statements to analyze to determine the best course of action."

Sam: "Considering the growth of your inventory, I assume your sales have increased substantially compared to previous years?"

b. Reality check:

Sam: "Let's take a closer look at your sales figures from last year to confirm that assumption. (sales figures reviewed) It appears that your sales have decreased slightly. Do you have any idea why that may be?"

Sarah: "I believe we were unable to trade effectively because of the lack of space in the warehouse."

c. Action:

Sam: "In this case, I recommend you create an inventory list to identify items that have not been moved in over nine months. Once we have that list, we can consider selling those items at a steep discount to move them out of the warehouse quickly. If we can do that, renting another warehouse right away may not be necessary. Can you work with your sales manager to evaluate the gross profit margin of those products and adjust the price accordingly? The goal is to price them at a level that covers variable operating expenses and results in some profit."

The meeting concluded with the action plan of identifying stagnant inventory. If these items occupy a significant amount of warehouse space, we'll need to perform another analysis to determine how much discount the company can offer to liquidate the inventory with a small profit. Sarah would be the one to decide how much profit she should accept.

Sarah later informed us of some unexpected findings. She discovered that around one-fourth of the inventory had stayed the same in the last 9 months. These inventories were in low demand, so freeing up space by selling them would allow her to increase the purchase of more popular stock. However, Sarah understood the inventories were not likely to be sold in a short period of time unless sales promotions were launched.

a. Expectation:

Sarah: "I'm hoping to sell the stagnant inventories to free up some warehouse space. By adjusting the prices, I want to maintain a healthy profit margin. Our typical gross profit margin is around 60%, but I can accept a lower gross profit margin for these stagnant items. The cost of these items is around $500,000. If we sell them at their regular price, we will make $1,250,000 ($500,000 / 0.4). Our gross profit would be $750,000 ($1,250,000 - $500,000) at the regular price. Can I afford to offer 50% off to the customers as a discount?

Sam: "The discount percentage should not be set arbitrarily. What is your desired operating profit from the sale of these inventories?"

Sarah: "These inventories are not as popular as they used to be, but they are not completely obsolete because I am sure some customers still want to buy them. What discount should we offer to earn at least $100,000 in net profit before tax?"

Sam: "It sounds like you won't need additional staff to sell these products quickly. What are the primary variable operating expenses associated with this sale promotion?"

Sarah: "I believe the primary variable expenses are advertising, merchant fees, shipping fees, and listing fees for Amazon."

Sam: "Based on our financial reports and historical data, advertising will likely account for about 3% of the sales, merchant fees about 3%, and Amazon listing fees about 8%. What about shipping fees?"

Sarah: "There are around 5,000 items identified as slow-moving in the inventory report. I think it's reasonable to budget around $30 per item for shipping costs."

b. Reality check:

Sam: "Great, I think this is all good information. Let's use our budgeted amount and check with your sales and warehouse managers.

Sarah told me the sales manager thought the advertising fee of $37,500, or 3% of the standard selling price, seemed too low for this sales promotion. They were confident to communicate with the prospective buyers with a budget of about $125,000 if Sarah wanted to liquidate the inventory quickly. The merchant fees and listing fees are reasonable. The good news is about the shipping cost. They weighed the slow-moving inventory and measured the dimension of them, and the shipping fee would be, on average, $25 per item, which is about $125,000 (5,000 units * $25 / unit)

Sam: "Great, I think you can do 24% off for each item, or a $294,944 discount in total, and you can still get about $100,000 in operating income for these inventories. Here is my analysis:

Sales before discount:	$1,250,000	
Discount	$(294,944.00)	24% off = (294,944 / 1,250,000)
Sales, net	$955,056	
cost	$500,000	
Gross profit	$455,056	47.65%
Advertising	$125,000	13.09%
Merchant fee	$28,652	3.00%
Amazon Listing	$76,404	8.00%
Shipping	$125,000	13.09%
Total variable operating expenses	$355,056	37.18%
Operating income	$100,000	10.47%

Figure 3.1

c. Action:

Sarah increased the advertising budget to promote discounted inventories. She followed the advice from her marketing manager to set the advertising budget of $125,000, which was about 3 times higher than the usual budget. Also, she took my advice of the discount of 24% off on those inventories.

A few months later, I was happy to hear that most of the slow-moving inventories were sold quickly and at a steep discount (about 24% off the regular price). The objective was to free up the warehouse space to trade other popular items. The additional profit from the stagnant inventories was indeed a bonus to Sarah already. I congratulated Sarah on her success.

I was pleased with the outcome and praised Sarah for her efforts. She felt more confident and empowered to make data-driven decisions and achieve better results in her business.

Takeaway

In the case study, we noted that the discount on the stagnant inventory should not be set arbitrarily. It should be based on the desired net operating income, the gross profit margin, and the variable operating expenses. If Sarah had just wanted to go with 50% off initially, she would have incurred an operating loss of about $193,000. The analysis had helped her avoid such loss but to free up the warehouse space by $100,000 net operating income.

Chapter 4- The ratio of labor to sales

Juan - a cleaning company's owner

I have a bookkeeping client who is providing house cleaning services. Their business is snowballing, thanks to the increased demand from short-term rental units and more households seeking help with cleaning.

After my team finished the monthly bookkeeping, the ratio of the profit and loss statement drew my attention. Here is the condensed version of the income statement (I have changed the number to protect my client's privacy)

XYZ Cleaning Services, LLC			
Income Statement			
		Year 20XX	% to sales
Sales		$ 1,000,000	
Personnel expenses			
Payroll	500,000		
Payroll tax	40,000		
Employee benefit	50,000		
Total personnel expenses		590,000	59.00%
Misc Overhead		200,000	20.00%
Total operating expenses		790,000	
Net profit before tax		$ 210,000	21.00%

Figure 4.1

a. Expectation

At first glance, the profit margin of 21% appears to be good. However, since this client operates his business as an LLC, and he and his spouse are off the payroll, the actual net profit before taxes would be less than 21% if they work full-time.

I discussed this issue with Juan, who confirmed that he and his spouse worked full-time for the business.

I explained to Juan that, based on industry standards, the budgeted labor cost-to-sales ratio should be 40% to 50%. However, as he and his spouse are also members of the LLC and work in the business, their guaranteed payments, similar to salaries, should be included in the labor cost to capture the time cost of the members.

After some calculations, assuming a fair value of $50,000 for each of Juan and his wife's guaranteed payments, the actual personnel expenses would be around $690,000, which includes $590,000 in regular labor costs and $100,000 in guaranteed payments.

b. Reality Check

The revised financial report will be as follows with the guaranteed payments of $100,000:

XYZ Cleaning Services, LLC			
Income Statement			
		Year 20XX	% to sales
Sales		$ 1,000,000	
Personnel expenses			
Payroll	500,000		
Payroll tax	40,000		
Employee benefit	50,000		
Gauranteed payment	100,000		
Total personnel expenses		690,000	69.00%
Misc Overhead		200,000	20.00%
Total operating expenses		890,000	
Net profit before tax		$ 110,000	11.00%

Figure 4.2

The labor cost-to-sales ratio is significantly higher than the budgeted range of 40% to 50%, at about 69%. It indicates that there may be underlying causes for the variance, which we must identify and address to improve the situation.

c. Action

Before taking action, we need to identify the root causes of the high labor-cost ratio. It requires a collaborative brainstorming session with Juan, who possesses the information on the daily operation of his business.

1. Pricing issue?

The most common symptom of a high labor cost ratio is undercharging clients. To address this possibility, I asked Juan if his company's rates were too low. He disagreed, stating that their fees were in line with their competitors in the local market. It was already a little too high.

To illustrate, he provided an example of a typical job where the company charges approximately $405 for 3 hours of work with 3 laborers. Based on his actual rate for the labor cost, which is about $15 per hour per employee, the total labor cost, before the payroll tax and employee benefit, for this job would be about $135 ($15/hour * 3 hours * 3 people).

The payroll tax and employee benefits are about 8% and 10% approximately, and thus the labor cost in the field will be about $135 *(1+18%) = $159

Additionally, Juan or his wife may spend an hour on average to communicate with the client and supervise the team, which equates to a rate of $24 per hour ($50,000 / 2,080 hours) times 1 hour. Therefore, the total labor cost for this job should be $183 ($159 +$24), representing about 45% ($183 / $405) of sales.

Their pricing formula seems reasonable, given the market and labor costs.

2. Labor cost issues?

Based on the example above, a typical 3-hour job is billed at $405, and the budgeted labor cost for this job should be $183, representing 45% of sales. However, the actual overall labor-to-sales ratio is 69%, indicating a labor cost issue.

There could be various reasons for the high labor cost, such as inefficient work processes, too much idle time, or overtime pay. When discussing these possibilities with Juan, he agreed these could be contributing factors.

i. Change order?

Juan also mentioned that sometimes jobs become more complicated than initially estimated, leading to more time spent in the field. I suggested offering clients a change order option in such situations, where the team could stop after the initially estimated time, explain which areas were not finished, and offer clients the option to add more hours to the job. Juan agreed to give this approach a try.

ii. Too many non-billable hours?

Reviewing the time sheets, Juan noticed that the labor crew sometimes only finished two 3-hour jobs in a workday, with about 2 hours lost in traffic. I suggested exploring better scheduling options to group jobs in the same neighborhood or hiring more part-time workers to minimize non-billable hours between jobs.

iii. Overtime pay?

In reviewing the payroll journals, some employees were paid overtime, which is 150% more than the regular hourly wage. I recommended hiring more part-time workers to reduce overtime pay expenses.

Takeaway

The labor-to-sales ratio is critical to service-based companies. The healthy ratio range should be between 40% to 60%, depending on the industries. Many LLC business owners are pleased with the labor-to-sales ratio before counting their work hours to the companies. They are not on the payroll. Sometimes, they may need to remember to include their time cost when giving the quotes to prospective clients. They tend to overestimate the profit of the LLC when they need to remember to include their guaranteed payments.

In this case study, we demonstrated the process of identifying the issue of high labor-to-sales ratio. We first estimated if the quotes to the customers were too low. Then we further examined the labor cost by reviewing the time sheets. Lack of changing orders, too many non-billable hours, and overtime rates are common root causes of incurring high labor costs. You can use these directions to examine your labor costs and evaluate if your company's labor cost to sales is reasonable.

Chapter 5- Marketing expenses

Many business owners understand the importance of budgeting marketing expenses. It's crucial to promote the business and scale the revenue. I have witnessed one of my clients grow his plumbing company from scratch to over $2 million in revenue in 2 to 3 years.

Santiago - an owner of a plumbing company

I still remember the day I first met Santigo at his apartment. He had just got started his plumbing company. As expected, he was the CEO, CFO, marketing manager, IT, and the only plumber in his company.

Although he was starting, he never overlooked the importance of having the books done monthly. He truly believed the financial statements could guide him to grow the company step by step. The bookkeeping fee to his business was a burden, but he saw it was an essential part of his business. I was grateful for his trust in my team to assist him.

He has a big vision to grow his business. He reinvested most of his profit back into the business by advertising his company to the local community. The marketing expenses were paid to 4 to 5 different marketing channels, including social media, newspapers, online classified, review-based websites, and yellow pages. I appreciated his entrepreneurial mindset and courage to scale his business.

However, marketing is not equal to gambling. I reached out to Santigo after the books were closed for the year. We perform "ERA" together.

a. Expectation

The annual marketing expenses were spent over $30,000 per year. I asked how much the marketing effort added new sales during the year. Santiago was proud to tell me his sales were grown from $50,000 per year to $150,000 per year. He told me the rate of return of his marketing expenses to new revenue ratio is 30%.

I further explained some sales were grown naturally because of the referral or current clients coming back for new services, although we were both certain the marketing efforts were the dominating factor of the growth. Even if all the latest sales come from the marketing efforts, could he track which way brought him most of the sales?

He was puzzled.

I urged him to start asking the new prospective clients how they found the company's contact and tracking the conversion rate in the current month. If the expectation of the marketing expenses to new revenue ratio is 30%, we should drop certain ineffective advertising below 30%. We made an appointment to meet again after the tracking exercise for about 30 days.

b. Reality Check

After a month, we met again, and he brought me the analysis below:

Advertising Media	Monthly Marketing Expenses ($)	Number of leads	Number of new customer	conversion rate	New Sales	Cost per new client
Social Media	1,300	75	1	1.33%	500	1,300
Newspaper	250	0	0	N/A	0	N/A
Online Classified	0	2	0	N/A	0	N/A
Reviewed-based website	750	60	18	30%	9,000	42
Yellowpages	200	0	0	N/A	0	N/A

Figure 5.1

He is a big believer in social media. He managed the campaign by himself. Although the conversion rate could have been better when only one new sale was generated from the social media platform, he explained that he could be in touch by email with 75 prospective customers who clicked the advertisement and left their email addresses. He obtained the prospective customers' email addresses because he developed a sales funnel in a landing page to send out digital vouchers. The potential from the email campaign is still huge, but just not seeing the result immediately in the month.

While I was convinced that social media helped build the audience group, which would be converted to new customers gradually, I wondered if it was the proper budget and time to invest $1,300 (about 10% of his revenue) in social media advertising platform monthly. There is no right or wrong. I defined this $1,300 as more for the brand equity development, which may be a low priority when his sales were about $150,000 annually. The company could see immediate sales growth if he maximized the investment in the marketing channel that was working for him at that moment.

c. Action

Santiago still believed in the long-term benefit of getting contacts from the advertising campaign on social media. He was convinced the amount was over his budget, slowing the business's growth. He reduced the budget for social media advertising to $300 per month. He increased the funding for the reviewed-based website to $2,000 per month, and he dropped the rest of the advertising in other media.

About a year later, we noted that his business exceeded 7 figures in revenue!

At that time, he was spending about $6,000 each month on the reviewed-based website with three different service locations. The two additional virtual offices pushed the search ranking up naturally. The return from the marketing effort was outstanding to expand their service territories. He was grateful the budget for the marketing effort was initially focused on the effective channel so that he could quickly generate more revenue and cash first. The success of this short-term goal helped him proceed to his next milestone - the brand he wanted to build.

Santiago continued optimizing the social media marketing strategy. The budget could be adjusted back to $1,000 monthly, as he had more cash flow from the growth. I still agree that building brand equity for long-term success is essential. He believed that was the right time to scale social media marketing. I had no objection because he has more marketing knowledge than I do. I was giving my advice by the number like a CFO of his company for the first milestone, and he should be the one to drive ultimately.

His judgment was correct; we noted that his revenue exceeded $2 million the following year. The email connection with the prospective customers strengthened the brand equity. Santiago often includes valuable content that lets the email recipients perceive his company as an expert in the plumbing industry. When people need services one day, they would naturally think about them and look for the contact from their email inboxes instead of searching online.

Chapter 6- Accounts Receivable Turnover

P ayment terms are a standard norm, but they come at a cost. It's not just the delay in receiving payment that affects companies, but also the time and effort spent following up on late invoices and the risk of turning the past dues into bad debts.

Jonathan - a consultation firm owner

One of my clients, a consulting firm, provided excellent services and had many clients, yet they experienced cash flow problems. Despite substantial net profits on paper, they regularly borrowed money to cover payroll, resulting in annual interest expenses of around $10,000.

a. Expectation

Jon admitted that their team spent much time chasing overdue payments when we discussed their cash flow issues. They believed their clients forgot about the bills rather than intentionally paying late. We discovered that the client's invoice terms were 30 days.

b. Reality Check

After finishing the bookkeeping, we calculated the Accounts Receivable

Turnover in Days, measuring how quickly a company collects customer payments.

The accounts receivable turnover ratio equals credit sales divided by the average accounts receivable. The formula is shown as follows:

Credit sales / Average Accounts receivable

$1,000,000 / (Accounts receivable at the year-end plus accounts receivable at the beginning of the year) / 2

$1,000,000 / $197,260 = 5.069

Accounts Receivable Turnover in Days = 365 / Accounts Receivables Turnover Ratio

Accounts Receivable Turnover in Days = 365 / 5.069

Accounts Receivable Turnover in Days = 72 days

We found that the client's Accounts Receivable Turnover in Days was 72, which explained their cash flow issues and the bad debts they had experienced.

a. Action

To address this, we suggested that the client contact customers with outstanding payments over 72 days and offer installment payment plans. We recommended offering a small discount of 5% for current customers who were willing to set up auto payments . Monthly installments would be taken automatically via ACH to settle the past-due accounts.

Additionally, we proposed adding a new paragraph to the client's engagement letter, informing future clients of the auto payment policy. We also suggested adding two more milestones to add the progress billings instead of billing the clients at the end of each project. It will relieve the pressure of labor costs.

Were these suggestions working?

Yes!

Although some clients initially questioned the auto payment option, most were happy to comply once they understood it was company policy. Some clients argued it was unusual to have auto-payments to a consultation company. Jon explained this was his firm's policy. That means Jon's firm can create a new norm!

Since many larger corporations, such as phone and utility companies, have used auto payments for over a decade, clients have become more comfortable with the idea. Only a few nowadays like to mail out checks anymore.

As a result, Jon improved their cash flow, minimized bad debts, reduced interest expenses, and reduced the time the accounts receivable clerk spent by 70%, saving between $60,000 and $100,000 per year.

Takeaway

The accounts receivable cycle should be evaluated regularly to develop procedures that can streamline the process, reduce internal time costs, and speed up the collection process. Do not be restricted by traditional practice. If you are confident in providing good services to your clients, you can design your billing schedule and how you collect the fees.

Chapter 7- Tax Projection

Although the tax filing is once a year, the tax projection and planning should never be made once a year. The cash in the bank may be misleading as this is the proceeds before tax. The estimated tax payments should be changed accordingly to avoid underpayment penalties and interest when the company grows. More importantly, a reserve for tax liabilities should be built during the year to ensure the cash flow is sufficient when the tax is due. It is not uncommon to see profitable businesses need to apply for installment plans as they don't have enough cash to pay for the tax liability.

Alex- a grocery wholesaler

I have a client, Alex, who is in a wholesale grocery business. His business grew a lot during the COVID, so even if the estimated taxes were paid in full, he would still owe tax because the estimated taxes were calculated based on the previous year's tax liability.

He was unaware of it, and whenever he saw cash in his bank account, he would either reinvest in the business or take it out for his personal investment. He may likely be suffering from the pressure of the tax balance due when he files a tax return in the following year.

Our team contacted him and performed the tax projection by "ERA" - expectation, reality check, and action.

a. Expectation

The estimated tax was calculated based on the previous year's tax liability. For example, in Alex's prior year's tax return, the tax liability was $400,000. To meet the Safe Harbor rule, he was required to pay at least 110% of the tax liability of the previous year in the current year to have penalty proof. That is $440,000 ($400,000 * 110%), thus each quarterly payment would be about $110,000 ($440,000 /4).

Based on his tax bracket, we devised an effective tax rate of 30%.

b. Reality check

We used the profit and loss statement of the first 7 months to project the tax liabilities. The annualized net profit before tax will be about $2,000,000, which boosted the effective tax rate up to 34%. The annualized net profit was estimated by the actual operating results of the first 7 months ($1,666,667 / 7) * 12 = $2,000,000.

The projected tax liability would be $680,000 ($2,000,000*34%). For simplicity, we skip the tax liability of the State in this case study.

If Alex continued the estimated tax payments of $110,000 per quarter, the tax balance due would be about $240,000 ($680,000-$440,000).

c. Action item:

Alex was unhappy to learn that more than the estimated tax payments would be needed to cover the tax liabilities. The additional cash flow appeared to be a lot. Still, the good news was he could choose to pay for the balance due of $240,000 by April 15 of the following year as long as he paid $110,000 quarterly to meet the safe harbor rule. More importantly, it was still early to prepare for the potential tax dues!

I asked him to save about $26,666 monthly for about 9 months (from Aug to Apr). He felt a little relieved when he did not need to pay it right away, and he felt a lot more prepared for the tax balance due next year with this mid-year projection. $26,666 was about 1% of his company's monthly revenue only. It was manageable to him as long as he set aside the money intentionally. I suggested he transfer the reserve to the money market account monthly. It would help him when he no longer sees this in the operating checking account.

We made an appointment to revisit the projection and see if there is any change in annualized profit at the year's end.

a. Expectation:

As discussed above, we projected the annualized net profit before tax to be $2,000,000.

b. Reality check:

When we finished the bookkeeping of November, the annualized profit was still about the same.

c. Action items:

If we did not do any tax planning, he would have a tax balance of

$240,000 by April 15 of the following year. He had prepared for it, and he had enough cash reserves for it. However, keeping more cash with the business as much as possible is always good. We went through the possible tax-saving strategies hoping to lower the taxable income.

Maximizing the contribution to the retirement plan

I asked Alex if he and his wife had contributed to 401(k). He said he contributed $9,000 only, but not his wife. He further explained he did not want to put her wife on payroll to additionally incur the payroll tax, even though his wife did work for the company part-time.

He was partially right about the payroll tax, which is about 15.3%, which would be incurred additionally for his wife's payroll. On the other hand, their taxable income in the joint individual income tax return would not be changed as the payroll deduction in the S-corporation would be the taxable income if his wife's W-2. However, the result will differ if his wife also participates in the 401(k) plan.

401(k) is an excellent strategy to defer the taxable income in the year his tax bracket is high. He would save tax immediately and use the savings to invest as if the government lent him money.

He won't be taxed until he distributes the money from the retirement account. By then, his effective tax rate could be lowered when he is in a lower tax bracket.

I recommended he first maximize his contribution. He was over 50 years old, and he could contribute up to $27,000. Since he contributed $9,000 only, he could further make a contribution of $18,000 to the 401(k) plan. Also, the company could match more. According to their plan, the company could match 100% of the contribution up to 3% of his compensation. The tax saving was approximately $6,500 additionally.

I also suggested he consider paying his wife $30,000 on the payroll.

First, it's required to pay the shareholders who work in the business a reasonable wage.

Also, there could be some tax savings in their situation. Here is the analysis

Tax saving from 401(k): $9,486 ($27,000 * 34% + 30,000*3%*34%)

Payroll tax: $4,590 ($30,000 * 15.3%)

Reduced tax benefit in Qualified Business Income deduction: 2,352 ($34,590*20%*34%)

Net saving: $2,544 ($9,486-4,590-2,352)

Overall, the additional tax saving in the above actions would be about $9,044 ($6,500+$2,544).

Putting their children on the payroll

After discussing paying his wife via payroll, I asked if his children worked for the company.

Alex has two sons who are college students. They helped the company remotely with the IT system and some clerical work during summer time. Alex did not put them on the payroll for the same reason of minimizing the payroll taxes. He thought there would be no change in the family income either as the deduction at the company's level became the income of his sons.

It was incorrect, though, as his sons have their own standard deductions on their tax returns even though they were still claimed as dependents in Alex's individual tax return. His sons were over 18 years old, which means each of his sons would report zero taxable income if the payroll were less than $30,000. The adjusted gross income would be $30,000 from W-2, but after the deferral of 401(k) and also the standard deduction of $12,950, the taxable income would be zero.

In short, paying payroll of $30,000 to each of his sons would allow the company takes the deduction of $60,000 while his sons do not need to report these as taxable income!

Tax saving in additional payroll of $60,000 = $20,400 ($60,000 *34%)

Payroll tax: $60,000 * 15.3% = $9,180

Reduced tax benefit in Qualified Business Income deduction: 4,080 ($60,000*20%*34%)

Net saving: $7,140

We had discussed additional possible tax planning regarding purchasing necessary equipment or vehicles, using his house as the venue for their upcoming company Christmas party, home use office, etc. The details of tax planning will not be discussed in this book. The objective is to let you understand that interim financial statements are helpful for your tax projection and tax planning.

Although only some of the strategies could apply to his situation, the tax projection using the interim financial statements helped him prepare the cash flow for the tax dues and implement specific, timely tax-saving measures by the year's end.

Chapter 8- Conclusion

I hope you get insights into using financial information to analyze and make informed decisions. The way we demonstrated from the above examples is not limited to the particular mentioned industries only; you can adopt the process of "ERA" to drive specific action plans for your own business.

After reading this book, you should be ready to start taking the role of CFO to perform a few fundamental analyses of the ratios in the financial statements. Can you see the numbers in the financial statements as opportunities to increase the cash now?

Timely financial reports are the critical foundation of ratio analysis. Suppose you have been letting your CPA catch up with the bookkeeping right before the tax filing deadline annually. In that case, I urge you to consider getting the monthly report instead. The expense you spend on the monthly bookkeeping fee will be like an investment. You should expect to see a return on it.

If you used to think that financial statements were for tax filing only, or you just paid attention to the bank's cash balance or the income statement's profit, I hope this book can change your mindset. You should be the primary user of the financial statements that guide you through building your business. I wish you the best, and enjoy your entrepreneurial experience!

Made in United States
Troutdale, OR
11/02/2023

14240878R00037